A Bug's World

March with the Ants

By Karen Latchana Kenney

Illustrated by Lisa Hedicker

Content Consultant

Clyde Sorenson, PhD

Professor of Entomology

North Carolina State University

magic wagon

visit us at www.abdopublishing.com

Published by Magic Wagon, a division of the ABDO Group, 8000 West 78th Street, Edina, Minnesota 55439.
Copyright © 2011 by Abdo Consulting Group, Inc. International copyrights reserved in all countries. All rights reserved. No part of this book may be reproduced in any form without written permission from the publisher.

Looking Glass Library™ is a trademark and logo of Magic Wagon.

Printed in the United States of America, North Mankato, Minnesota.
042010
092010

Text by Karen Latchana Kenney
Illustrations by Lisa Hedicker
Edited by Amy Van Zee
Interior layout and design by Becky Daum
Cover design by Craig Hinton

Library of Congress Cataloging-in-Publication Data
Kenney, Karen Latchana.
  March with the ants / by Karen Latchana Kenney ; illustrated by Lisa Hedicker.
    p. cm. — (A bug's world)
Includes bibliographical references and index.
ISBN 978-1-60270-788-7
1. Ants—Juvenile literature. I. Hedicker, Lisa, 1984- ill. II. Title.
QL568.F7K44 2011
595.79'6—dc22

                    2009052917

Table of Contents

Social Insects

March, march, march. Ants crawl in and out of an anthill. From above, their bodies make a rippling patch of brown on the ground.

Ants are social insects. They live together in groups called colonies. A single colony can have hundreds or thousands of ants.

More than 10,000 kinds of ants live on Earth. Most live in nests under the earth. Tunnels connect their underground rooms. Other ants live inside trees. Carpenter ants chew tunnels inside wood. Weaver ants glue tree leaves together with silky webbing.

Some ants do not live in nests. Army ants are always on the move. The colony stays a few days in one place. Then it moves on.

Ants do not live in water, and they do not live in very cold places. Like humans, the insects can be found almost everywhere on Earth's land.

Ant Jobs

Ants in a colony help each other. Each ant has a special job. Most ants are workers. These ants find food for the whole colony. They also take care of the nest. They are all female, but they do not lay eggs. Down in the nest, there is another female—the queen. Her only job is to lay eggs.

Most colonies have just one queen. One of the workers' most important jobs is to feed and protect the queen. If the queen dies, the colony cannot survive.

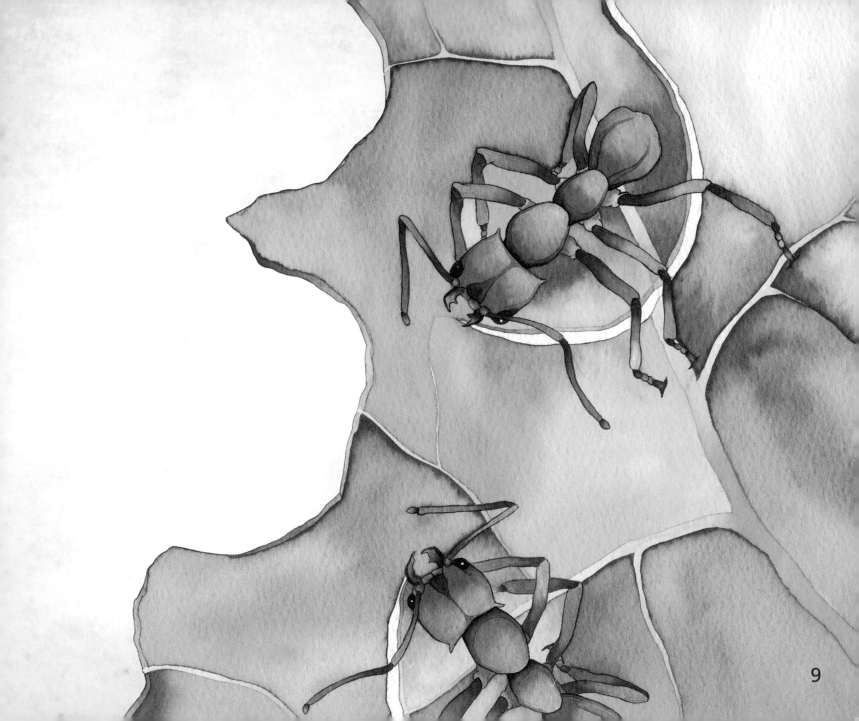

The males are the last kind of ant in a colony. Their only job is to mate with the queen so she can lay eggs. The males and queen leave the nest to mate.

Only the young queen and males have wings. They group together to make a swarm. The mating flight happens in the air. Then they drop to the ground. Soon after mating, the males die.

After mating, a queen pulls off her wings. She may do so with her jaws or her legs. Or she rubs them against a rock or other object.

Hatching, Changing, Growing

At first, an ant egg is so small it can barely be seen without a microscope. But it grows fast. In just a few days, the egg hatches. A larva comes out.

Lots of larva together are called larvae. They look like small, white worms. The worker ants feed the larvae. The larvae grow. In a few weeks, they change again.

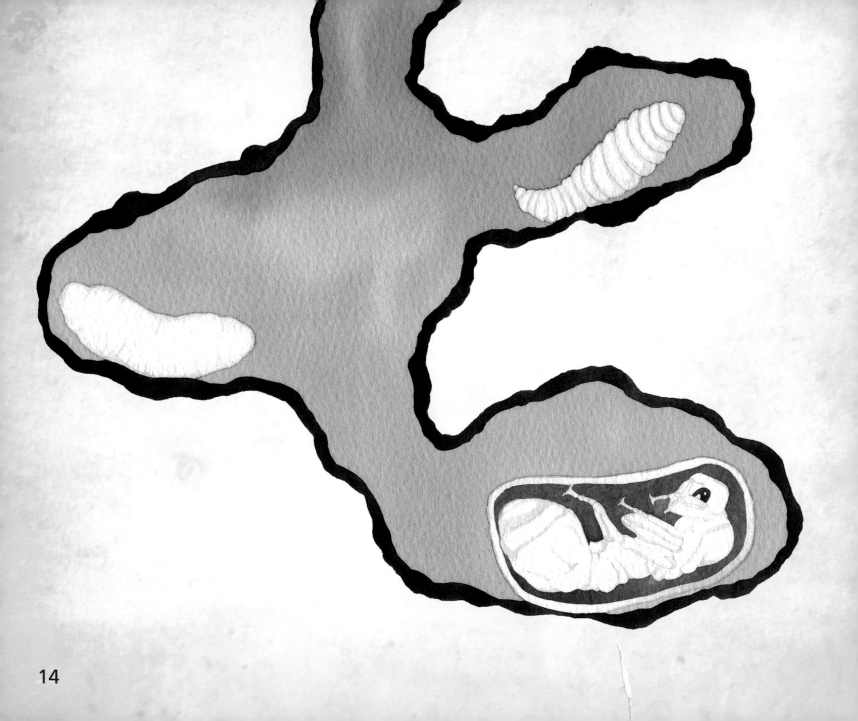

In most cases, a larva spins a silk cocoon around its body. Inside, the creature changes into a pupa. It looks like a small, white ant. After a few weeks, the pupa is done changing. When it comes out from the cocoon, the ant is an adult.

Finding Food, Staying Safe

Most likely, the adult ant is a worker. *March, march, march.* The insect leaves the nest to gather food. Different kinds of ants gather different foods. Many eat bugs or plant parts. The ant's antennae, mandibles, and eyes help it find food or stay safe.

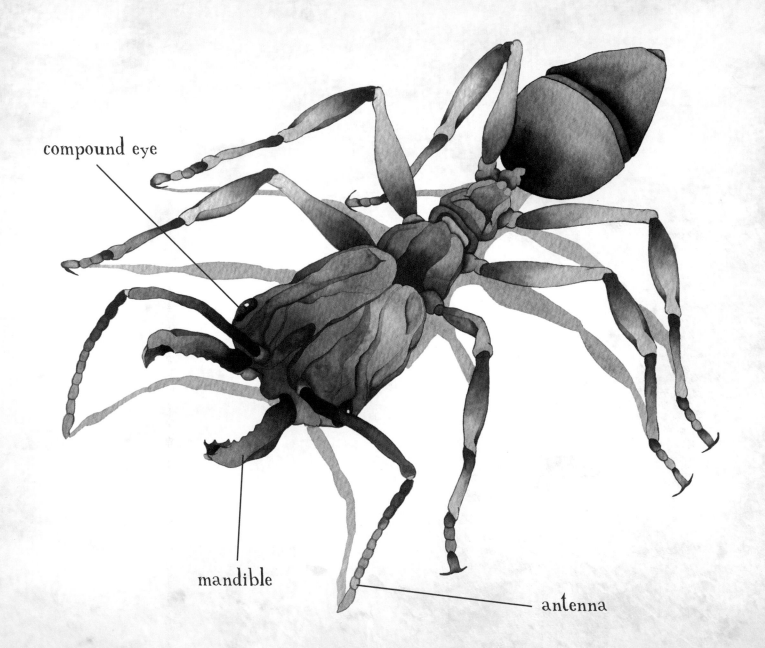

compound eye

mandible

antenna

17

An ant's two long, bent antennae wave in the air. They touch the ground. They touch food. They touch other ants. The ant uses its antennae to smell, touch, and taste.

Smell is especially important. Ants' bodies give off different kinds of smells. If an ant senses danger, it will release a special smell. The smell is like an alarm that warns the rest of the colony. Ants also give off smells to lead other ants in the colony to food.

Near its mouth, the ant's mandibles move from side to side. These important tools help an ant hold things and catch food.

Leaf-cutter ants use their mandibles to carry leaf pieces back to their nest. There, they chew up the leaves. The wet, mushy leaves are good for growing fungus—a type of living thing like mold or mushrooms. The ants feast on the fungus.

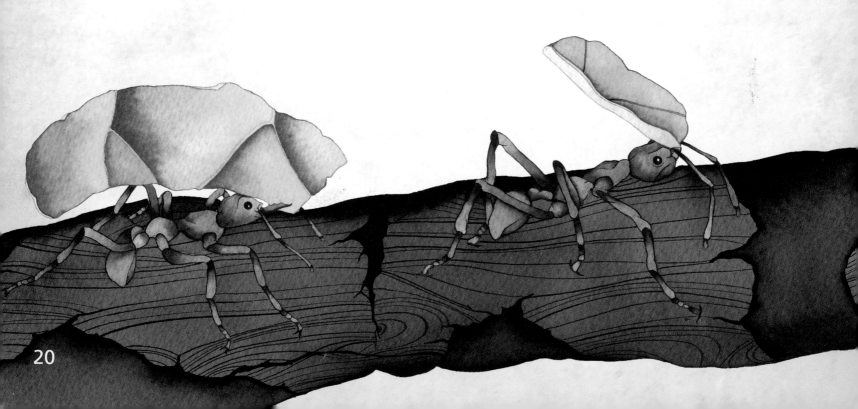

The sharp mandibles can also be weapons.
Ants use them to bite their enemies.

21

Two big eyes bulge from the sides of an ant's head. These are compound eyes. They are made of many tiny lenses. Each lens takes in just a part of an image, like a piece of a puzzle.

An ant's eyes let it see fast-moving things, but only close-up. The insects can see hungry birds swooping down or frogs leaping close.

Some ants have three simple eyes in between their compound eyes. These help the ant see light and shadows.

Ants may see the flash of an anteater's tongue. But they can't get away fast enough! The large animal licks them up, hundreds at a time.

Some ants can fight back. A sharp stinger sticks out from the back of an ant's body. The ant pushes it into an enemy's skin. Poison shoots out the stinger. Some kinds of ants may swarm in a large group and attack together.

The Colony Continues

In the winter, ants stay deep in their nests. They go into a kind of deep sleep. In the spring, the colony wakes up. Soon after, the queen will lay more eggs.

The workers get busy. *March, march, march.* They gather food. They feed the young. The colony continues to grow.

Ants live longer than most other insects. Though males only live a few months, queens can live more than 20 years. Most workers live less than a year.

An Ant's Body

An ant's body has three main parts: the head, the thorax, and the abdomen. The insect's skeleton is a hard, outer casing. It protects the ant's soft body like a suit of armor.

The gaster is the end of an ant's abdomen. The petiole is like a thin waist between the thorax and the abdomen.

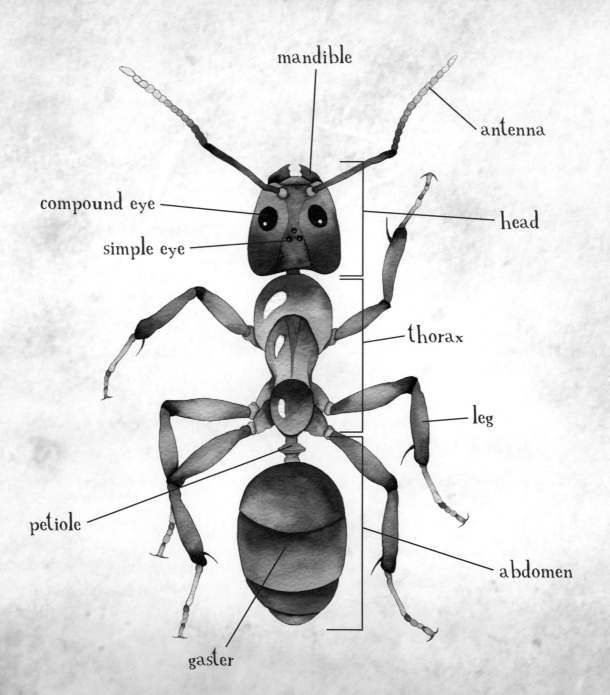

mandible

antenna

compound eye

head

simple eye

thorax

leg

petiole

abdomen

gaster

A Closer Look

Observe an Ant Colony

What you will need:

- magnifying glass
- notebook
- pencil
- watch or clock

Worker ants leave the nest to find food. Ants you see above ground are worker ants.

Ask an adult to help you find some ants outside. See if you can find the entrance to their nest. Use your magnifying glass to watch the ants come out and go into the nest. Try to stay out of their path. Watch the ants for ten minutes. Record what you see.

Watch these things:
- What do the ants look like?
- What are the ants carrying?
- How do the ants move?
- How many ants can you count?

Ant Facts

- Ants can come in many colors! Most ants are yellow, red, black, or brown. But some can even be orange or purple.
- Army ants can attack birds and small animals. The ants move in such a big group that they are difficult for other animals to fight off.

Glossary

abdomen—the back part of an insect's body.

antenna (an-**TEH**-nuh)—one of the two long, thin body parts that sticks out from an insect's head and is used to feel and smell.

cocoon—a silk bag a larva spins around itself. Inside the cocoon, the larva changes into an adult insect.

colony—a population of plants or animals in a certain place that belongs to a single species.

compound eye—an eye made up of thousands of lenses, with each one taking in a piece of an image.

mandibles—the jaws of a bug.

swarm—a large group of insects. To swarm also means to gather into a large group.

thorax— the middle part of an insect's body.

On the Web

To learn more about ants, visit ABDO Group online at **www.abdopublishing.com**. Web sites about ants are featured on our Book Links page. These links are routinely monitored and updated to provide the most current information available.

Index